TAURUS

THE ARTFUL ASTROLOGER

TAURUS

Lee Holloway

Gramercy Books
New York • Avenel

To my children

A Friedman Group Book

Copyright ©1993 by Michael Friedman Publishing Group
All rights reserved.

This 1993 edition is published by Gramercy Books,
distributed by Outlet Book Company, Inc.,
a Random House Company, 40 Engelhard Avenue,
Avenel, New Jersey 07001.

Printed and bound in Singapore

Library of Congress Cataloging–in–Publication Data

Holloway, Lee.
        The artful astrologer.   Taurus / by Lee Holloway.
              p.   cm.
        ISBN 0-517-08248-9
        1. Taurus (Astrology)   I. Title.
     BF1727.2H65   1993
     133.5'2—dc20   93-24869
                                              CIP

8 7 6 5 4 3 2 1

CONTENTS

6   Introduction

14   The Planets

16   The Zodiac Signs

20   Your Sun Sign Profile

25   Compatibility With the Other Signs

44   Birthdays of Famous Cancers

48   About the Author

Photo Credits

Symbolic rendering of a seventeenth-century astrologer.

INTRODUCTION

I s astrology bunk, or is there something to it? If astrology is utter nonsense, why have so many of the world's finest thinkers, including Johannes Kepler, Copernicus, Isaac Newton, Carl Jung, and Goethe, turned to astrology for information and guidance over the centuries?

Some people may scoff when astrology is mentioned, but even these skeptics are usually inquisitive about their signs. Whenever I attend a dinner party, I ask the host not to mention that I am an astrologer—at least not until dessert—because the conversation invariably turns to astrolo-

In the middle ages, the wealthy consulted astrologers regularly.

gy. When people learn that I am an astrologer, they first try to get me to tell them about their signs and what lies in store for them. Then, in a subtle way, they bring up the next bit of business, which usually concerns a loved one. Finally, as you've probably guessed, they want to know whether the two signs get along.

We humans are an inquisitive lot—we are eager to learn more about our friends, family, lovers, and employers. Astrology is one way to satisfy that natural curiosity.

In the not too distant past, only royalty, heads of state, and the very rich consulted with astrologers; such consultation was a privilege of the elite. Today, astrology is a source of information and fascination for millions; astrological columns can be found in major newspapers and magazines all over the world.

Astrology is not a form of magic. It is a science. Put simply, it is a practical application of astronomy that links the stars and planets with our daily lives. A horoscope is a picture of the stars and planets at a given time, such as that of a person's birth. By examining each planet's position and the relationships of all of the planets to each other at a specific moment, an astrologer can determine your basic personality or predict a general course of events. Perhaps the noted Swiss psychologist Carl Jung summed up the concept of astrology best when he said, "Whatever is born or done at this moment, has the qualities of this moment in time." Astrologers form a continuous link with the past, and each human being, although unique, is part of nature and the universe.

Unfortunately, some people have the misconception that astrology dictates who they are and how their life has to be.

This chart dates back to fourteenth-century Italy. The inside circles represent the element, ruling body part, and orientation of each respective sign.

Medieval illuminated manuscript of biblical characters observing the stars.

Nothing could be further from the truth. Astrology does not remove our free will; it simply points out our basic nature and how we are likely to react in certain circumstances. Astrology indicates strengths and weaknesses, talents and abilities, difficulties and opportunities. It is always up to the individual to use this information, and to live his or her life accordingly, or to disregard it.

Like other sciences, astrology's origins date back thousands of years. There is evidence that primitive peoples recorded the phases of the Moon by carving notches on reindeer bones, and that they may have linked the Moon's movement with the tides, or the snow's melting in spring with the rising of the constellation now known as Aries. As early as 2000 B.C., astrologers were using instruments—carved out of granite or fashioned from brass or copper—to observe and calculate the positions of constellations. These calculations were surprisingly accurate, even by today's standards.

Over time, astrological calculations were refined and the planets were named. The Babylonians were the first to describe the natural zodiac, and their first horoscope dates back to 409 B.C. Centuries ago, people began to examine the stars' potential impact on human emotions, spirit, and intellect. Today, astrology is so deeply embedded in our culture and language that we rarely give it a second thought. The

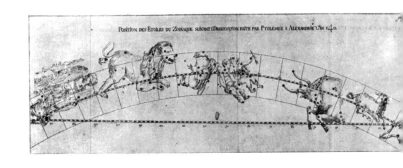

The twelve zodiacal constellations as drawn according to Ptolemy's descriptions.

days of the week , for example, have their roots in astrology. Sunday is derived from "Sun Day," Monday from "Moon Day," Tuesday from "Tiwe's Day," Wednesday from "Woden's Day," Thursday from "Thor's Day," Friday from "Frigga's Day," and Saturday from "Saturn's Day." Lunacy, which originally referred to so-called full-moon madness, now encompasses all varieties and forms of mental illness.

Before we begin, I'd like to touch upon one final point. Throughout this book, you'll see references to "rulers." A ruler, in astrological terms, has the same meaning as it does in human society; "ruler" refers to the planet that governs or co-governs an astrological sign (see pages 14–15) or to the constellation rising at the birth of a person or event. Everything has a moment of birth: people, places, profes-

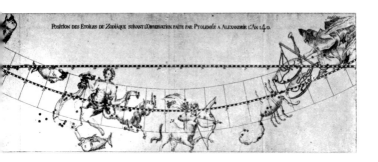

POSITION DES ÉTOILES DU ZODIAQUE suivant l'Observation faite par Ptolémée a Alexandrie l'An 140.

sions, even ideas; it would take volumes to show you what persons, places, and things your sign rules, but a small sampling has been included here. For example, different parts of the body have rulers, and that body part is often a point of strength and weakness. Gemstones and colors have also been assigned to each sign, although there are varying opinions about the validity of these less important areas. (It should also be noted here that the gemstone assigned to a particular sign does not correspond to the birthstone assigned to that month.) Generally, however, colors and gemstones are said to reflect the specific energy of each sign.

May *The Artful Astrologer* enlighten and entertain you.

Lee Holloway

THE PLANETS

The **SUN** symbolizes the life force that flows through everything. It rules the sign of Leo and represents ego, will, identity, and consciousness.

The **MOON** symbolizes emotions and personality. It rules the sign of Cancer and represents feeling, instinct, habit, childhood, mother, sensitivity, and receptivity.

MERCURY symbolizes the mind and communication. It rules the signs of Gemini and Virgo and represents thought, learning, communication, reason, speech, youth, and perception.

VENUS symbolizes love and attraction. It rules the signs of Taurus and Libra and represents harmony, values, pleasure, comfort, beauty, art, refinement, and balance.

MARS symbolizes action and drive. It rules the sign of Aries and represents energy, the sex drive, initiative, the ability to defend oneself, resilience, and conflict.

JUPITER symbolizes expansion and growth. It rules the sign of Sagittarius and represents higher thought and learning, principles, beliefs, optimism, abundance, idealism, and morals.

SATURN symbolizes universal law and reality. It rules the sign of Capricorn and represents structure, discipline, limitation, restriction, fear, authority figures, father, teachers, and time.

The nine planets that comprise our solar system: Mercury, Venus, Earth, Mars, Saturn, Jupiter, Uranus, Neptune, and Pluto.

URANUS symbolizes individuality and change. It rules the sign of Aquarius and represents intuition, genius, insight, reform, unconventionality, and freedom.

NEPTUNE symbolizes compassion and spirituality. It rules the sign of Pisces and represents the search for the divine, intuition, dreams, illusion, imagination, and confusion.

PLUTO symbolizes transformation and regeneration. It rules the sign of Scorpio and represents power, death and rebirth, the subconscious, elimination, obsession, and purging.

THE ZODIAC SIGNS

J ust as there are twelve months in the year, there are twelve astrological signs in the zodiac. The word "zodiac" comes from the Greek *zoidiakos,* which means "circle of animals" and refers to a band of fixed stars that encircles the earth. The twelve signs are divided into four elements: fire, air, earth, and water. The three signs within an element share many similarities, but each sign in the zodiac is unique. The following section is a brief summary of the qualities of the signs born under each element. (The terms "positive" and "negative" as they are used here describe qualities, and are not judgments.)

The fire signs are Aries, Leo, and Sagittarius. They are termed positive and extroverted. They are warm, creative, outgoing, expressive, idealistic, inspirational, and enthusiastic.

The air signs are Gemini, Libra, and Aquarius. They are termed positive and extroverted. They are social, outgoing, objective, expressive, and intellectual.

The earth signs are Taurus, Virgo, and Capricorn. They are termed negative and introverted. They are practical, conservative, reserved, traditional, and deliberate.

The water signs are Cancer, Scorpio, and Pisces. They are termed negative and introverted. They are sensitive, emotional, imaginative, and intuitive.

The fire signs:

Aries   Leo   Sagittarius

The air signs:

Gemini   Libra   Aquarius

The earth signs:

Taurus   Virgo   Capricorn

The water signs:

Cancer   Scorpio   Pisces

Tau

ℛ

Symbol: Bull

Planetary ruler: Venus

Element: Earth

Rules in the body: Throat

Day of the week: Friday

Gem: Emerald

Color: Bright green

Key words: I have

r u s

YOUR SUN SIGN PROFILE

The Taurean symbol is the Bull, and like the Bull, Taureans can be stubborn. But the Bull also exemplifies this sign's great strength and determination. Phrases like "solid as a rock" or "dependable as the day is long" were probably coined to describe people born under this sensual sign. Consistent, reliable, and practical, Taurus is the literal bedrock of the zodiac. Taurus co-rules the earth and is the creative, persistent force that shaped the natural wonders of our world. With production credits like these underscoring your potential accomplishments, little can stop you from achieving your goals. Taureans are built for endurance, not speed, so it may take you a bit longer to succeed, but you will eventually do so.

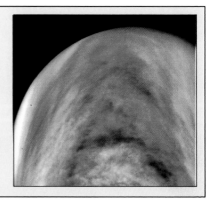

ASTRONOMICAL FACT

Venus, planetary ruler of Taurus, is almost the exact size of the Earth. Because Venus is covered in dense clouds, it has a beautiful, soft appearance and is brightly lit. Its axis rotation is backward, and it takes this planet almost 243 days to orbit the Sun.

Taurus is a sign that has great creative potential. Venus, this pleasure-loving sign's planetary ruler, governs the arts in all its forms. Taureans are patient, determined, easy-going, loyal, and loving, and they also often have the ability to create works of art and literature that can stand the test of time. Shakespeare was a Taurus, as were Socrates, Balzac, Tchaikovsky, Brahms, and Robert Browning. And these are just a few of the many talented individuals with whom you share your sign. So don't think for a minute that Taurus' steady or cautious approach implies a lack of intelligence. Nothing could be further from the truth.

Taureans need security, and this is reflected in their key words "I have." Financial security is a primary concern. Taureans often panic if their financial security is uncertain or in jeopardy; consequently, they are quite adept at saving money. Taureans often aren't really happy until they can indulge themselves and those they love with some of life's fineries. This is a sign that loves good food and drink, as well as comfortable surroundings and clothing.

When it comes to career, Taureans' keen eye for value and strong interest in money often leads them to work in the business world as investment bankers and managers, tellers, or financial planners. A Taurean may also find professional fulfillment in the arts. There are many Taureans who are famous artists, art dealers, jewelers, musicians, singers, actors, actresses, dancers, and sculptors, including Bing Crosby, Martha Graham, Ella Fitzgerald, Jack Nicholson, and Frank Stella. Since Venus usually gives Taureans pleasing personalities that make them very attractive to other people, it's easy to see why many Taureans are naturally financially successful. They possess a magnetic quality that brings out the best in other people, who in turn help them achieve their goals.

SOME CITIES RULED BY TAURUS

Dublin, Ireland
Mantua, Italy
Minneapolis, Minnesota
Palermo, Italy
Rhodes, Greece
St. Louis, Missouri

As regards love and romance, the Taurean energy can easily be summed up by one name: Valentino. Not all Taureans boast the dark good looks of silent-screen legend Rudolph Valentino, who was a Taurus, but they do know how to make love. Unless you have something causing a short circuit in the rest of your astrological makeup, you make love with artistic skill. In this department, the Taurean credo is simple: "Don't rush; there is so much to be enjoyed."

When it comes to relationships, Taureans believe in always giving their absolute best, and this philosophy is a good indicator of how they expect to be treated in return. Because Taureans are faithful, reliable, warm, and caring, and have good

The famous Gateway Arch in St. Louis, Missouri.

old-fashioned values about loyalty and commitment, one would have to go far to find a better partner than a Taurus.

In general, Taureans need to become less attached to material things and less possessive of other people. If you are a typical Taurean, you may also have to remember that everyone has a right to an opinion; after all, variety is the spice of life! Since Taureans have so many wonderful talents and qualities, learning these few lessons is a small price to pay for happiness.

*Venus rules Taurus and the arts, so it's no wonder that dance greats
such as Fred Astaire and Judith Jamison (both born May 10),
and Martha Graham (May 11) were born under this sign.*

COMPATIBILITY WITH THE OTHER SIGNS

In nature, some elements are more compatible and blend more easily than others, like fire and air, and earth and water. The same holds true in astrology. Therefore, some astrological signs naturally interact more harmoniously than others.

In this section you will learn how Taurus tends to relate to other signs. It provides guidelines to the potential strengths and weaknesses of a relationship between two signs. But remember, these are only guidelines. In the final analysis, the choice is yours.

As an earth sign, Taurus is most compatible with the other earth signs, Virgo and Capricorn. The natural rapport of the earth signs is due to their many emotional and intellectual similarities.

In nature, "earth gives water form, and water nourishes earth." The same is true in astrology. This is why earth and water signs are basically compatible. The water signs Cancer and Pisces are very compatible with Taurus. Although Scorpio is also a water sign, it

SOME PROFESSIONS RULED BY TAURUS

architect
art dealer
artist
auctioneer
banker
bank teller
builder
cabinetmaker
candy maker
carpet layer
cashier
dancer
financier
jeweler
leather manufacturer
musician
sculptor
singer
treasurer

*Sugar Ray Leonard is proof that Taureans generally possess strength
of physique as well as of character.*

Barbra Streisand has directed and starred in many of her own films —a real coup in male-dominated Hollywood— evidence of her sign's great determination.

is Taurus' opposite in the zodiac, so the relationship would be more challenging than a relationship with one of the other water signs.

The fire signs Aries, Leo, and Sagittarius are not as compatible with Taurus as the water and earth signs, for fire signs are extroverted and tend toward spontaneous behavior and speech, while Taurus is introverted, slow-moving, and prefers action based upon a well-thought-out plan.

The air signs Gemini, Libra, and Aquarius are the least compatible with Taurus, as air signs are too changeable for the steadfast Bull. Taurus is also a bit of a homebody, and the air signs generally prefer to be on the go.

SINCE TAURUS RULES THE THROAT, IT'S NO WONDER SO MANY TAUREANS ARE TALENTED SINGERS

Theodore Bikel
James Brown
David Byrne
Cher
Joe Cocker
Rita Coolidge
Judy Collins
Perry Como
Bing Crosby
Bobby Darin
Sheena Easton
Ella Fitzgerald
Peter Gabriel
Engelbert Humperdinck
Janet Jackson
Billy Joel
Grace Jones

Bono

Willie Nelson
Roy Orbison
Iggy Pop
Bobby Rydell
Bob Seger
Pete Seeger
Kate Smith
Hank Snow
Barbra Streisand
Pete Townsend
Randy Travis
Ritchie Valens
Frankie Valli
Fats Waller
Steve Winwood
Stevie Wonder
Tammy Wynette

VIRGO AND TAURUS

 Virgo (August 24–September 22) and Taurus are an excellent combination. Taurus is calm, steady, patient, and very strong, which can help balance high-strung Virgo. Virgo's quick intellect will fascinate Taurus, who tends to think and act slowly and deliberately. These two signs are reliable and will be able to count on each other for support. They also share a strong drive regarding work. Virgo is the workaholic of the zodiac, often putting in long hours. Security-minded Taurus, who also has an eye on earnings, will appreciate Virgo's efforts. Together, these two can strive to achieve a mutual goal without there being a lot of tension about the time work takes away from their relationship.

CAPRICORN AND TAURUS

 Capricorn (December 22–January 19) and Taurus are also a fine combination. As earth signs, they are practical, conservative, and security-minded. They are both gifted with business sense, so financial arguments should be few. Taurus has great stamina and persistence but may need someone else to get the ball rolling, so Capricorn's restless, action-oriented energy is a nice complement. Capricorn is more emotionally reserved than affectionate Taurus, so Taurus' warmth and amiability may offset Capricorn's aloof personality. All in all, these two should be happy together.

TAURUS AND TAURUS

 Two Taureans can form a successful relationship because of their similar natures; after all, it's easier to understand someone who is so much like yourself. But similarity can be too much of a good thing for a pair of the same sign, since they share the same strengths and weaknesses. Because two Taureans are equally determined and stubborn,

Kinderdyk, Holland

there could be a problem with the give-and-take necessary to maintain a relationship. These two simply may find it hard to compromise. On the whole, however, the basic warmth and affection they share can do much to mediate such problems.

CANCER AND TAURUS

Cancer (June 22–July 23) and Taurus share a deep love of family and a need for security. Cancer is the most sensitive sign of the zodiac and experiences emotional ups and downs on a daily basis, while Taurus takes matters in stride and is very even-tempered. Taurus' stable nature can provide temperamental Cancer with much-needed support. Cancer, on the other hand, is intuitive and caring, and thus able to respond quickly to Taurus' needs. Both signs are possessive and deeply committed to those they love. The pairing of Cancer and Taurus is a natural one, so these two should be able to forge a wonderfully comforting union.

PISCES AND TAURUS

 Pisces (February 19–March 20) and Taurus make a highly suitable-match. Pisces is gentle, intuitive, and imaginative, but often lacks direction and stability. Taurus can be the answer to Pisces' prayers in such matters, since direction and stability are part and parcel of the Taurean nature. Taurus is a no-nonsense, down-to-earth individual, and Pisces, with a natural nurturing ability and a rich imagination, can be a soothing and enriching force in Taurus' life. There is also a great potential for an unspoken rapport between these two—one that they would be hard put to explain to others or even articulate themselves.

SCORPIO AND TAURUS

 Scorpio (October 23– November 21) is Taurus' polar opposite in the zodiac, and the old saying that opposites attract certainly rings true here. Each sign possesses and can offer qualities that the other lacks. Scorpio is intense and private, while Taurus is easygoing and open. Taurus is practical and concerned mainly with the here and now, while Scorpio is emotional and interested in feelings and life's deeper mysteries. Both are determined and inflexible signs, so it may be difficult for them to compromise when opposing views arise—and compromises will have to be made

The marriage between Candice Bergen (Taurus) and Louis Malle (Scorpio) is a fine example of the way two opposites can interact. Here the signs' shared determination and goal orientation are obvious: Malle is a successful film director (Au Revoir Les Enfants, Atlantic City, Murmur of the Heart, My Dinner with André), and Bergen is a successful actress, currently starring in the hit television series Murphy Brown. Malle's Scorpio intensity and ability to deal with powerful emotions is evident in his films. As Murphy Brown, Bergen is constantly coping with one problem or another, but seems to be the stabilizing factor in each situation, a typical Taurean role. Malle and Bergen keep their private lives out of the public eye, so it's difficult to accurately speculate about the status of their marriage, but from what appears in the press the two seem to be happy together.

TAUREAN ACTORS KNOWN FOR PLAYING CHARACTERS OF GREAT STRENGTH

Lionel Barrymore
Cher
Gary Cooper
Daniel Day-Lewis
Albert Finney
Henry Fonda
Charles Grodin
Dennis Hopper
Glenda Jackson
Jessica Lange
Al Pacino
Anthony Quinn
Jimmy Stewart
Debra Winger

Jack Nicholson

Michelle Pfeiffer

because of some very basic personality traits. Still, this can be a dynamic pairing if both people are mature enough to accept and appreciate these differences.

ARIES AND TAURUS

A union between Aries (March 21–April 20) and Taurus brings together some very different energies. Aries is quick, impatient, and impulsive, while Taurus is deliberate, patient, and has an itinerary. Aries is naturally competitive and combative, while Taurus is serene and dislikes confrontations. This pairing can produce some interesting sparks, since it brings together Venus, ruler of Taurus, and Mars, ruler of Aries; these two planets represent the natural attraction between the sexes. An Aries-Taurus combination is to some degree the result of this natural attraction, but there will be some friction and a need for adjustment. However, Taureans would benefit from an Arian boost of energy to get them going, while Taurus' strong will could help Aries finish what he or she starts.

LEO AND TAURUS

Leo (July 24–August 23) and Taurus also make an unusual combination, although, curiously enough, the two are often attracted to each other. Both Taurus and Leo are determined and opinionated, which obvi-

Katharine Hepburn (Taurus) and Spencer Tracy (Aries) are a fine example of a Taurus-Aries union. On-screen, there was a natural excitement between the strong-willed duo as they bantered with and cajoled each other in one movie after another. Off-screen, the two had a romantic relationship for more than twenty-five years. Tracy's slew of pet names for Hepburn, such as "Coo-Coo the Bird Girl" and "Madame LaFarge," is evidence of his sign's playfulness, while Hepburn's unwavering dedication to Tracy demonstrated her sign's strength and deeply loyal and nurturing nature. In the early days of their relationship, Hepburn stood by Tracy despite his drinking and related disappearances, and in the years before his death, she stopped acting to devote herself fully to nursing the ailing actor.

ously can work against them when they disagree. Taurus loves to have and to hold, while Leo loves to have and to spend. Both like objects of good quality and love to share good times, but Leo may seem too lavish and impractical to earthy Taurus. Taurus is conservative and cautious, while Leo is expansive and enjoys taking risks. There are more differences than similarities here, which could be draining for both signs over the long term. A Leo-Taurus union is one of those relationships that will require a lot of continuous adjustment.

SAGITTARIUS AND TAURUS

 Sagittarius (November 22–December 21) and Taurus are very different signs, but a relationship between the two brings together very harmonious ruling planets, Venus and Jupiter. Taurus is controlled, sensible, and focuses on the day-to-day, while Sagittarius is expansive, idealistic, and thinks of the future. At first glance one would think these differences would create friction, but both signs have easygoing, loving natures. Sagittarius is also highly flexible and willing to compromise, which would balance Taurus' tendency toward obstinacy. Taurus often gets into ruts, and Sagittarius is just the one to get the Bull to step

Bing Crosby possessed that wonderfully mellifluous Taurean voice.

out of these routines. Sagittarius loves freedom, however, and possessive Taurus may have trouble coping with this. Although there are some essential differences here, Taurus and Sagittarius could make some interesting music together.

GEMINI AND TAURUS

 Gemini (May 22–June 21) and Taurus are an unlikely combination. Gemini is intellectual and thrives on change, while Taurus is interested in reality, not ideas, is consistent, and has difficulty coping with change. Taurus may see Gemini as superficial and flighty, while Gemini may think Taurus is a stick-in-the-mud. Gemini likes to soar and explore; Taurus likes both feet to be on the ground and prefers the tried-and-true. With so little in common, this certainly would be a difficult match to maintain, even though Taurus could provide Gemini with stability, and Gemini could bring Taurus a host of new friends, experiences, and ideas. Everyone has their idea of a perfect relationship, so for some, this quirky combination just may be what they're looking for.

Taureans are nurturing and have a calming effect upon others, qualities embodied by Audrey Hepburn, who worked ardently to bring comfort to children in impoverished countries around the world.

LIBRA AND TAURUS

 Of all the air signs, Libra (September 23–October 22) has the greatest affinity with Taurus, for the two signs share a ruling planet, Venus. However, Libra loves to socialize, meet new people, and intellectualize, while Taurus loves a familiar routine and prefers intimate gatherings with good friends. These two may share a mutual love of music and art, although their tastes will probably differ. Taurus loves and lives in a sensual way, while Libra is cool and loves on a more intellectual level. Libra also loves with refinement and grace, which may seem too aloof and detached for practical Taurus. Taurus and Libra make quite interesting bedfellows and will have an unusual relationship if they get together.

AQUARIUS AND TAURUS

 Aquarius (January 20–February 18) and Taurus make an odd pair, for they

Honoré de Balzac

**TAUREANS WHO
COULD REALLY TURN
A PHRASE**

David Attenborough
L. Frank Baum
Peter Benchley
Charlotte Bronte
Robert Browning
Bruce Chatwin
Joseph Heller
David Hume
Immanuel Kant
Edward Lear
Harper Lee
Anita Loos
Ngaio Marsh
Thomas Pynchon
William Shakespeare
Studs Terkel
Robert Penn Warren
George F. Will
Paul Zindel

Jimmy Stewart's complete devotion to his wife, Gloria, in their marriage of almost forty years is testimony to his sign's great loyalty to loved ones.

go together about as well as oil and water. Aquarius, the rebel of the zodiac, thrives on chaos and change. Taurus is traditional and often makes changes only after tremendous pressure has been applied. Aquarius loves the new, while Taurus needs the familiar. Taurus personifies the saying "If it ain't broke, don't fix it," while Aquarius needs to reinvent the world constantly. This association is dubious, but if the two get together, the relationship certainly will never be tepid.

Both signs are stubborn, so giving in and giving up would be difficult. Obviously, this pairing is not for the faint of heart.

Remember, astrology's compatibility guidelines do not mean that one sign can't have a good relationship with another. They merely indicate areas where there is potential for harmony and areas that will require patience, adjustment, and acceptance.

Discord makes peace-loving Bulls see red, and on her album Rhythm Nation, *Taurus Janet Jackson showed her true astrological colors.*

BIRTHDAYS OF FAMOUS TAUREANS

Queen Elizabeth

April 20

Jessica Lange

April 21

Charles Grodin • Anthony Quinn • Tony Danza
Queen Elizabeth II • Charlotte Brontë • Iggy Pop

April 22

Jack Nicholson • Nikolai Lenin • Immanuel Kant
Aaron Spelling • J. Robert Oppenheimer

April 23

William Shakespeare • Ngaio Marsh • Roy Orbison
Sandra Dee • Shirley Temple Black

April 24

Barbra Streisand • Shirley MacLaine • Jill Ireland
Robert Penn Warren • Eric Bogosian

Ella Fitzgerald

Al Pacino

April 25

Al Pacino • Oliver Cromwell • Ella Fitzgerald • Guglielmo Marconi

April 26

Bobby Rydell • Anita Loos • Carol Burnett
John James Audubon • David Hume

April 27

Sheena Easton • Anouk Aimée • Samuel Morse • Jack Klugman

April 28

Jay Leno • Lionel Barrymore • Ann-Margret • Harper Lee

April 29

Hirohito • William Randolph Hearst
Celeste Holm • Duke Ellington
Daniel Day-Lewis • Michelle Pfeiffer

Duke Ellington

April 30

Willie Nelson • Cloris Leachman
Eve Arden • Jill Clayburgh

May 1

Rita Coolidge • Kate Smith
Judy Collins • Jack Paar • Joseph Heller

James Brown

May 2

Benjamin Spock • Bing Crosby • Theodore Bikel

May 3

Doug Henning • Engelbert Humperdinck
James Brown • Frankie Valli • Pete Seeger

May 4

Audrey Hepburn • Roberta Peters • Randy Travis
Maynard Ferguson • Tammy Wynette • George F. Will

May 5

Alice Faye • Karl Marx • Michael Palin • Tyrone Power

May 6

Rudolph Valentino • Sigmund Freud • Orson Welles
Willie Mays • Randall Jarrell • Bob Seger

Orson Welles

May 7

Johannes Brahms • Peter Ilyich Tchaikovsky • Eva Perón
Johnny Unitas • Robert Browning • Gary Cooper

May 8

David Attenborough • Peter Benchley • Thomas Pynchon

May 9

Albert Finney • Mike Wallace • Billy Joel • Hank Snow
Candice Bergen • Glenda Jackson

May 10

Fred Astaire • Judith Jamison • Bono

May 11

Irving Berlin • Mort Sahl • Robert Jarvik
Martha Graham • Salvador Dali

Florence Nightingale

Billy Joel

May 12

Burt Bacharach • Edward Lear • Steve Winwood
Frank Stella • George Carlin
Florence Nightingale

May 13

Stevie Wonder • Ritchie Valens • Bea Arthur • Joe Louis
Peter Gabriel • Bruce Chatwin

May 14

George Lucas • David Byrne • Gabriel Fahrenheit • Bobby Darin

May 15

L. Frank Baum • Richard Avedon • Jasper Johns • Paul Zindel

Dennis Hopper

May 16

Henry Fonda • Studs Terkel • Gabriela Sabatini
Janet Jackson • Yannick Noah • Liberace

May 17

Debra Winger • Dennis Hopper • Sugar Ray Leonard
Christian Lacroix • Archibald Cox

Grace Jones

May 18

Margot Fonteyn • Frank Capra • Perry Como

Cher

May 19

Ho Chi Minh • Nora Ephron • Grace Jones • Pete Townshend

May 20

Socrates • Jimmy Stewart • Cher • Honoré de Balzac • Joe Cocker

May 21

Raymond Burr • Fats Waller • Andrei Sakharov

ABOUT THE AUTHOR

Lee Holloway has been a practicing astrologer with an international clientele for more than fifteen years. The author of a series of comprehensive astrology engagement calendars, she has hosted her own television and radio programs, including her current show on KABC Talk Radio in Los Angeles. A Sagittarius and the mother of three, she lives in Woodland Hills, California.

PHOTO CREDITS

Archive Photos: p. 44 bottom left
© Larry Busacca/Retna Ltd.: p. 43
© Dave Chancellor/Alpha/Globe: p. 44 top left
© Bill Davila/Retna Ltd.: p. 47 bottom left
© Michael Ferguson/Globe Photos: p. 34 bottom
FPG International: pp. 41, 44 right, 45 right, 46 bottom right
© F. Garcia/Stills/Retna Ltd.: p. 33 left
© Steve Granitz/Retna Ltd.: p. 46 left
© S. Halleran/Allsport: p. 26
© Sandra Johnson/Retna Ltd.: p. 47 top left
© Breck P. Kent: p. 18
Movie Star News: pp. 24, 27, 33 right, 34 top, 36, 38, 40, 42, 46 top right,
Courtesy Museum of Natural History, Department Library Services: pp. 9, 12–13
NASA: pp. 15, 20
New York Public Library: pp. 6, 7, 10
© Alan Nyiri/FPG International: p. 23
Photofest: p. 28
© David Redfern/Retna Ltd.: p. 45 left
© Govert de Roos/Retna Ltd.: p. 47 right
© Steve Vidler/Leo de Wys Inc.: p. 30